EARLY BIRD

Fun Songs for Kids

12 VERY EASY PIANO SOLOS WITH TEACHER DUETS

CONTENTS

ISBN 978-1-70513-760-4

HAL•LEONARD®

Visit Hal Leonard Online at
www.halleonard.com

Contact us:
Hal Leonard
7777 West Bluemound Road
Milwaukee, WI 53213
Email: info@halleonard.com

In Europe, contact:
Hal Leonard Europe Limited
42 Wigmore Street
Marylebone, London, W1U 2RN
Email: info@halleonardeurope.com

In Australia, contact:
Hal Leonard Australia Pty. Ltd.
4 Lentara Court
Cheltenham, Victoria, 3192 Australia
Email: info@halleonard.com.au

Preface

Fun Songs for Kids is a mix of familiar favorites and new original compositions with lyrics and teacher duets for every song. The *Early Bird* level is perfect for beginners, and features a horizontal format, keyboard charts, large font size and note names printed inside the note heads. My hope is that *Fun Songs for Kids* will encourage students to play and sing, which promotes musical playing, ear training, and, most of all, enjoyment!

– Jennifer Linn

Jennifer Linn is a multi-talented pianist, composer, arranger and clinician. As a clinician, she has presented workshops, master classes, and showcases throughout the United States, Canada, and India. From 2009–2019 she held the title of Manager–Educational Piano for Hal Leonard LLC, the world's largest print music publisher. Ms. Linn is the editor and recording artist for the award-winning *Journey Through the Classics* series and the G. Schirmer Performance Editions of *Clementi: Sonatinas, Op. 36, Kuhlau: Selected Sonatinas,* and *Schumann: Selections from Album for the Young, Op. 68.* Her original compositions for piano students frequently have been selected for the National Federation of Music Clubs festival and other required repertoire lists worldwide.

Ms. Linn's teaching career spans more than 30 years and includes independent studio teaching of all ages, as well as group instruction and piano pedagogy at the university level. She received her B.M. with distinction and M.M. in piano performance from the University of Missouri–Kansas City (UMKC) Conservatory of Music where she was the winner of the Concerto-Aria competition. She was named the Outstanding Student in the Graduate piano division and given the prestigious Vice Chancellor's award for academic excellence and service. In 2013, the University of Missouri–Kansas City Conservatory of Music and Dance named Ms. Linn the UMKC Alumnus of the year. In 2020, she was presented with the Albert Nelson Marquis Lifetime Achievement Award as a leader in the fields of music and education.

About the Jennifer Linn Series

Each book in the *Jennifer Linn Series* will feature a wide variety of either original piano compositions or popular arrangements. The music is written in a **progressive order of difficulty**, so pianists of any age can enjoy their music with the added benefit of a gradual challenge as they advance to each new piece in the book. The *Jennifer Linn Series* includes five levels:

Early Bird books feature music notation on the grand staff with the note names printed inside the note heads. The font size is large, and the book is in a horizontal format. Optional teacher or parent duets (in small font) are included. *Early Bird* books are designed for beginners, helping them gain confidence in their ability to read music.

Easy Elementary features the simplest, single-note Grand Staff notation in a large font size. This level is for the beginning pianist just learning to read notes on the staff and is printed in a regular vertical format.

Elementary+ books include melody with harmony for both hands and include more rhythm choices and a larger range of keys. This level is for the progressing student who has two to three years of experience.

Easy Intermediate is similar to Hal Leonard's *Easy Piano* level, but includes pianistic accompaniment patterns and more advanced rhythm notation as required.

Intermediate+ is for advancing pianists who have progressed to the Piano Solo level and enjoy lush accompaniments and stylistic original compositions and arrangements.

4

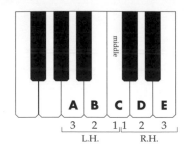

Backpack Blues

Words and Music by
Jennifer Linn

Cheerfully

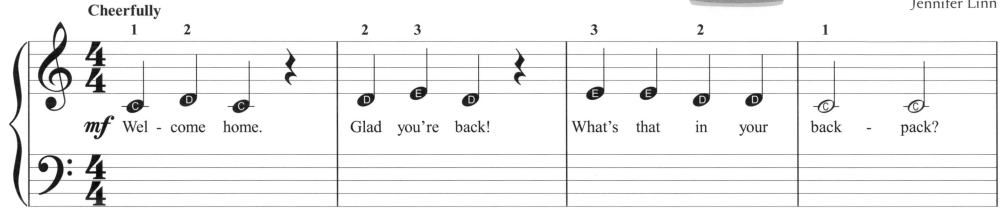

mf Wel - come home.   Glad you're back!   What's that in your back - pack?

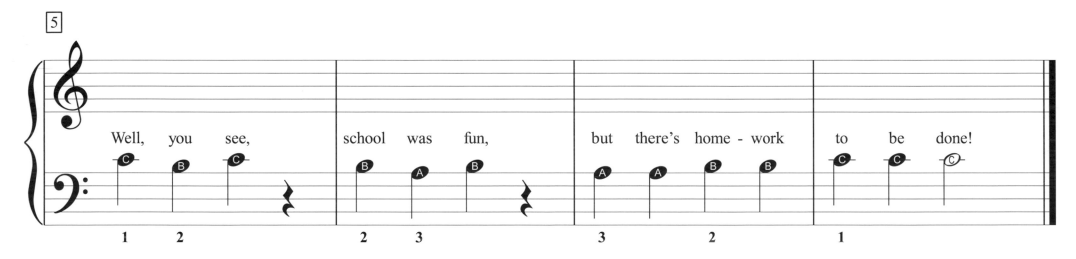

Well, you see,   school was fun,   but there's home - work   to be done!

Accompaniment (Student plays one octave higher than written.)

Cheerfully

Volga Boat Song

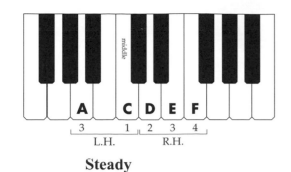

Russian Folk Song
Arranged by Jennifer Linn

Steady

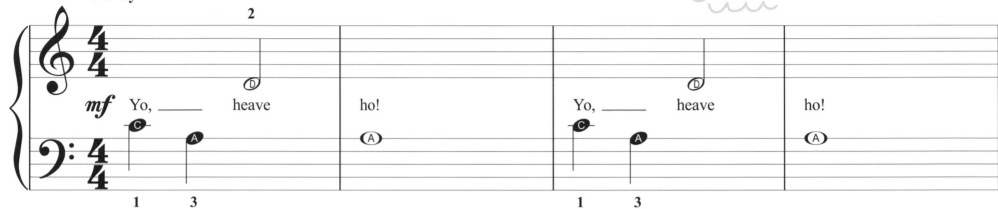

Yo, _____ heave ho!   Yo, _____ heave ho!

Once more, once more, yo, _____ heave ho!

Accompaniment (Student plays one octave higher than written.)
Steady

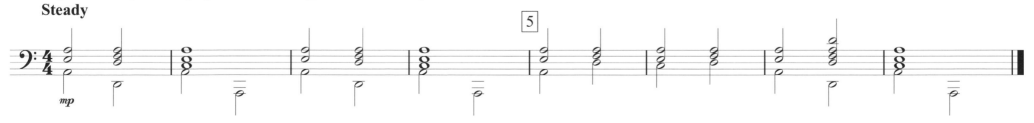

6

Attic Stairs

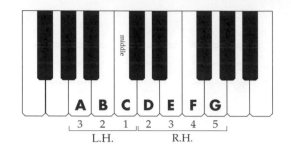

Words and Music by
Jennifer Linn

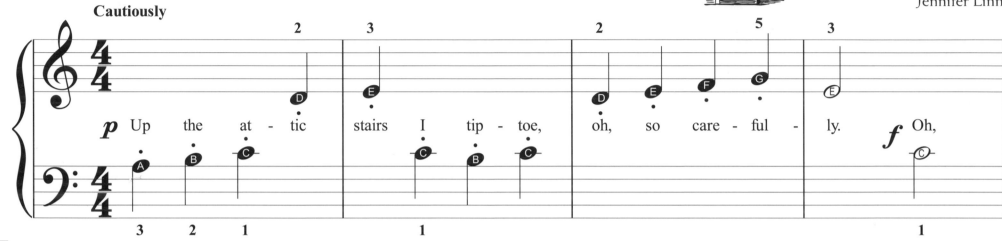

Cautiously

p Up the at - tic stairs I tip - toe, oh, so care - ful - ly. *f* Oh,

what's that sound? Turn a - round! Nev - er mind, it's on - ly me!

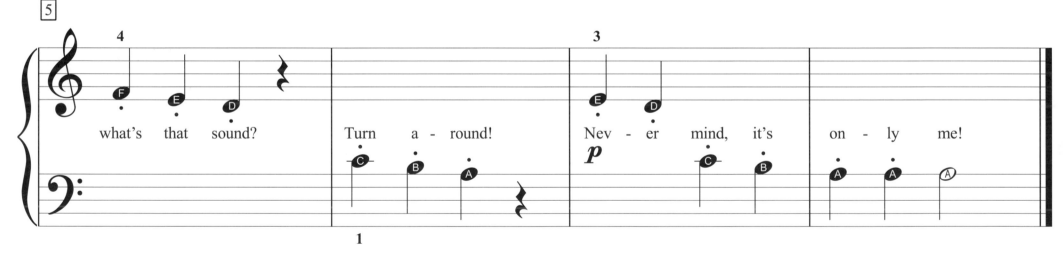

Accompaniment (Student plays one octave higher than written.)

Cautiously

Hush, Little Baby

Carolina Folk Lullaby
Arranged by Jennifer Linn

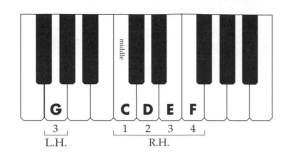

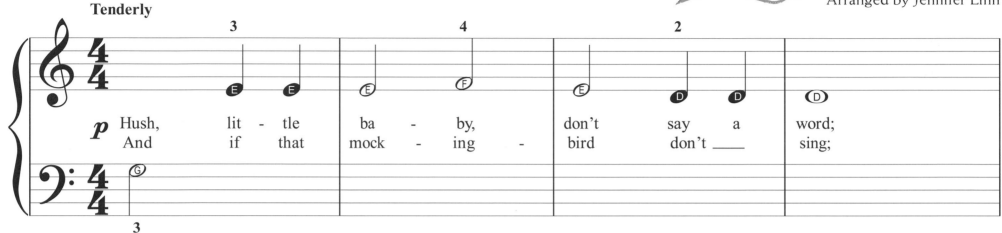

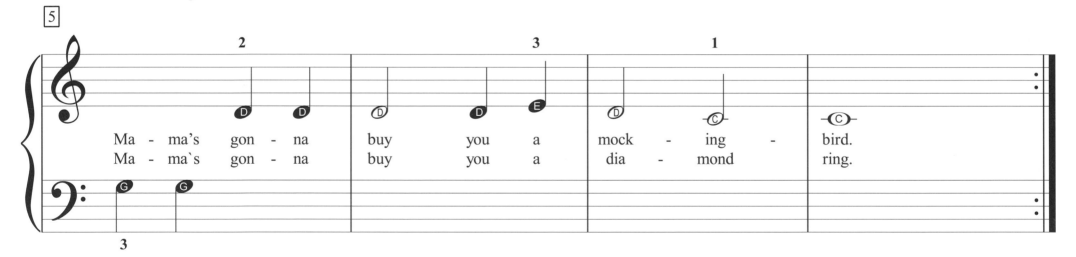

Accompaniment (Student plays one octave higher than written.)

8

Song of the Buffalo

Words and Music by
Jennifer Linn

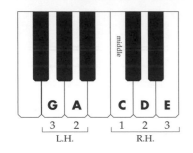

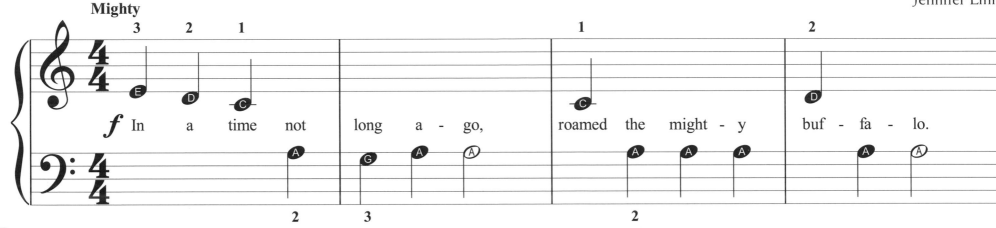

Mighty

In a time not long a - go, roamed the might - y buf - fa - lo.

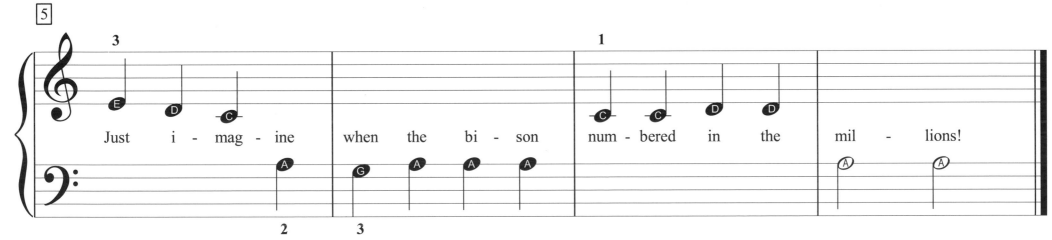

Just i - mag - ine when the bi - son num - bered in the mil - lions!

Accompaniment (Student plays one octave higher than written.)

Mighty

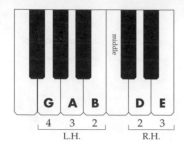

Mountain Train

Words and Music by
Jennifer Linn

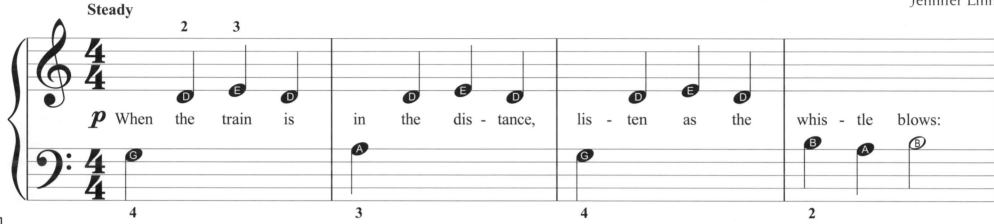

Steady

When the train is in the dis - tance, lis - ten as the whis - tle blows:

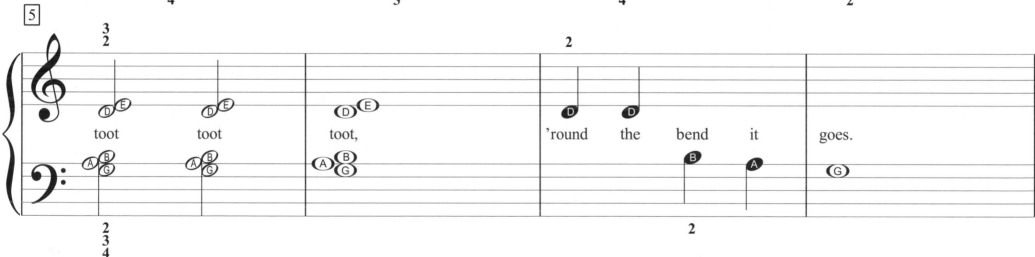

toot   toot   toot,   'round the bend it   goes.

Accompaniment (Student plays one octave higher than written.)

Steady

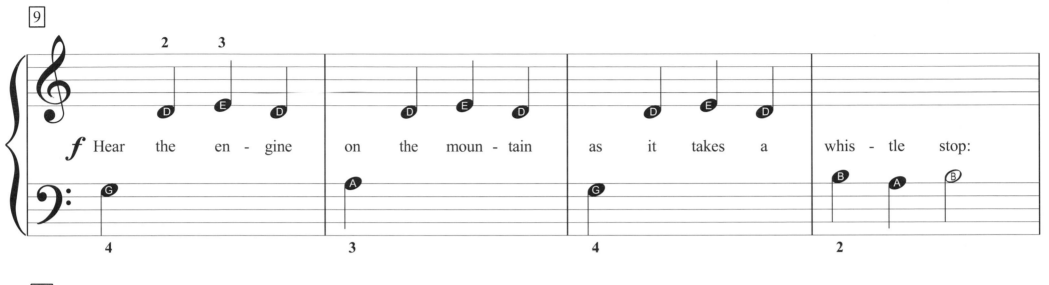

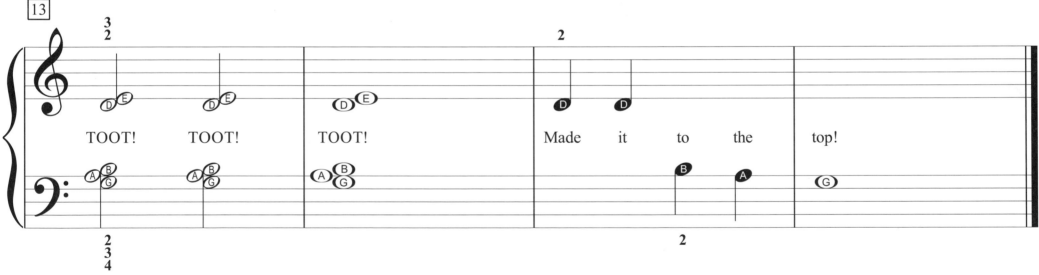

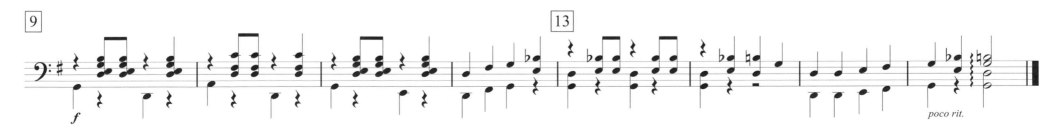

Fading Moon

Words and Music by
Jennifer Linn

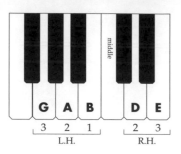

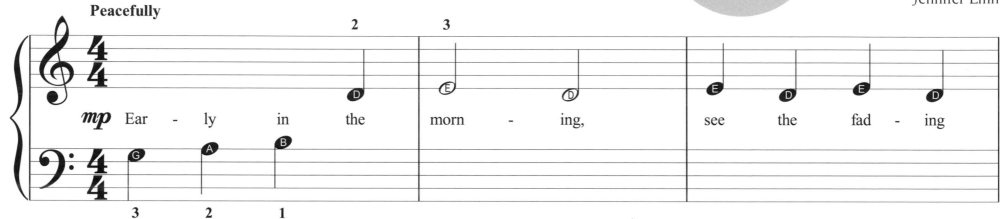

Peacefully

mp Ear - ly in the morn - ing, see the fad - ing

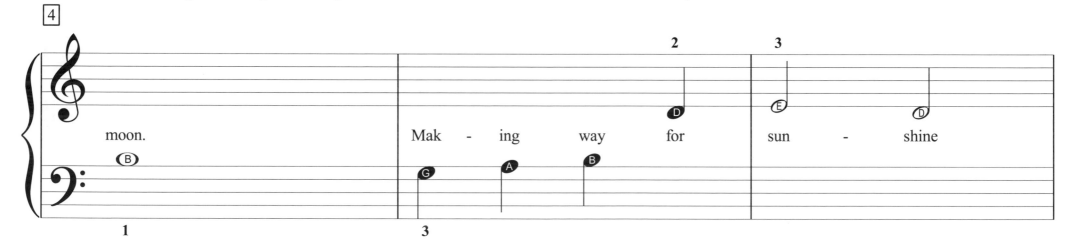

moon. Mak - ing way for sun - shine

Accompaniment (Student plays one octave higher than written.)

Peacefully

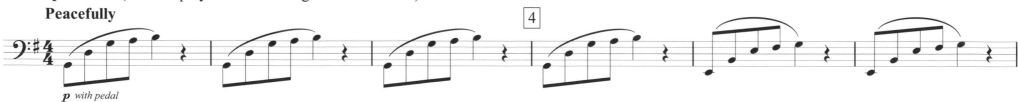

p with pedal

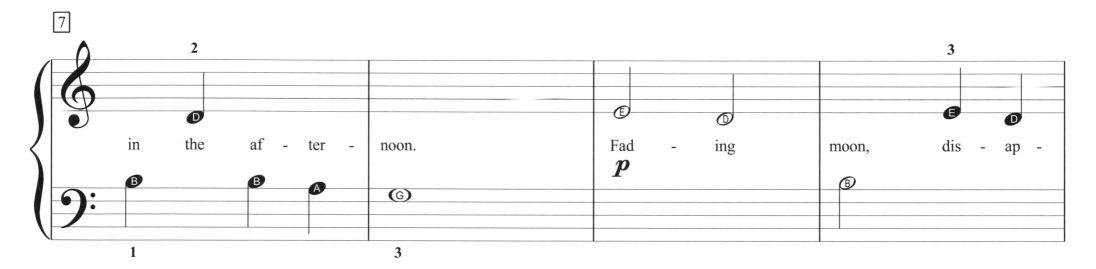

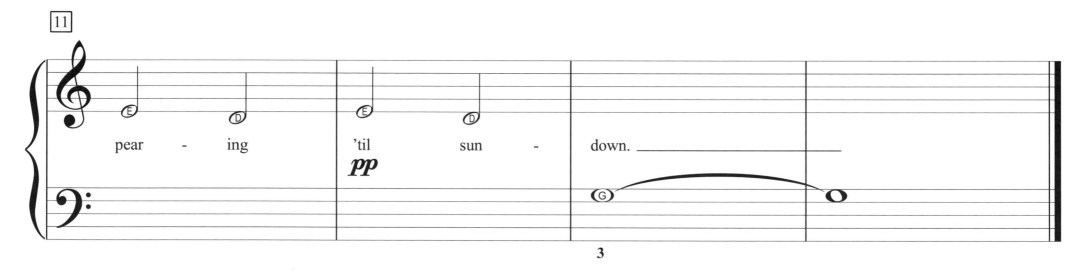

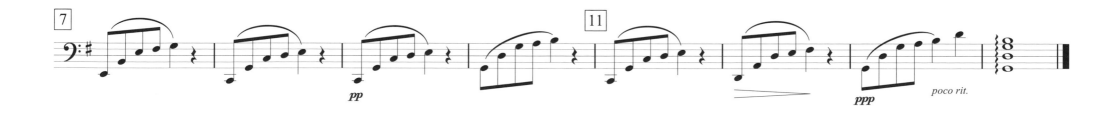

Bingo

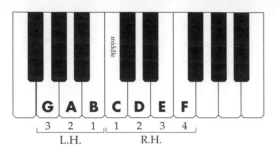

Traditional
Arranged by Jennifer Linn

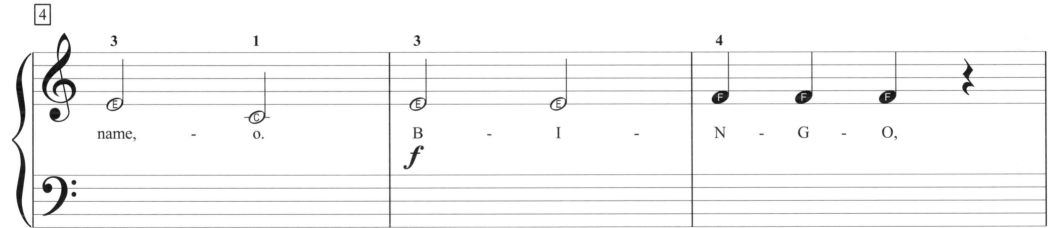

Merrily

mf There was a farm-er had a dog and Bin-go was his name, -o. B - I - N - G - O,

Accompaniment (Student plays one octave higher than written.)

Merrily

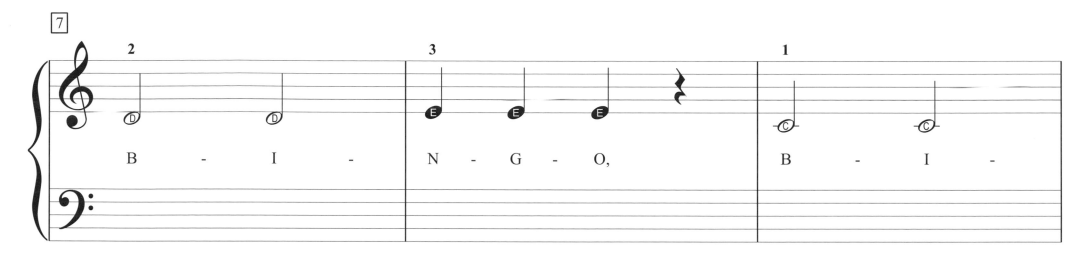

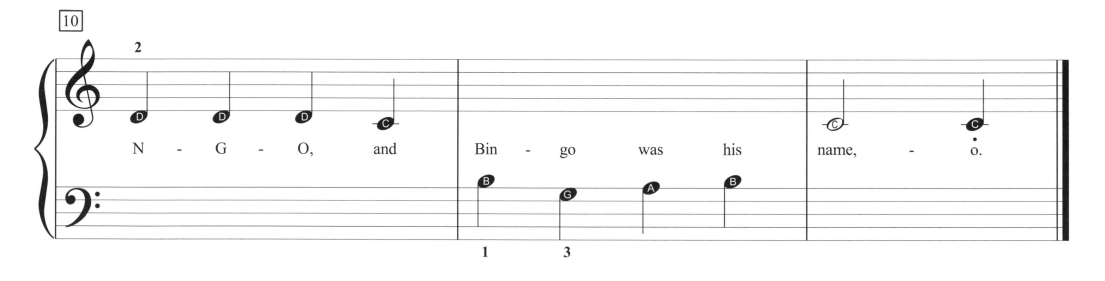

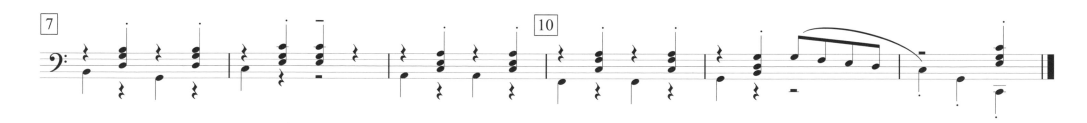

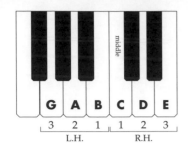

16

The Bear Went Over the Mountain

American Folk Song
Arranged by Jennifer Linn

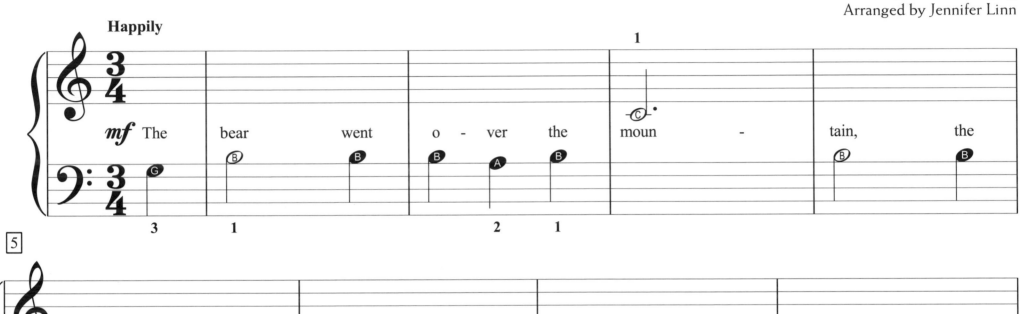

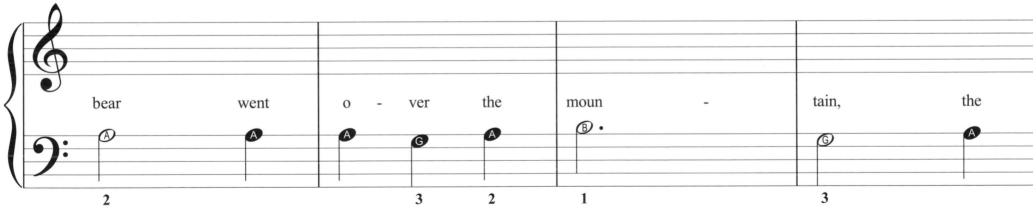

Accompaniment (Student plays one octave higher than written.)

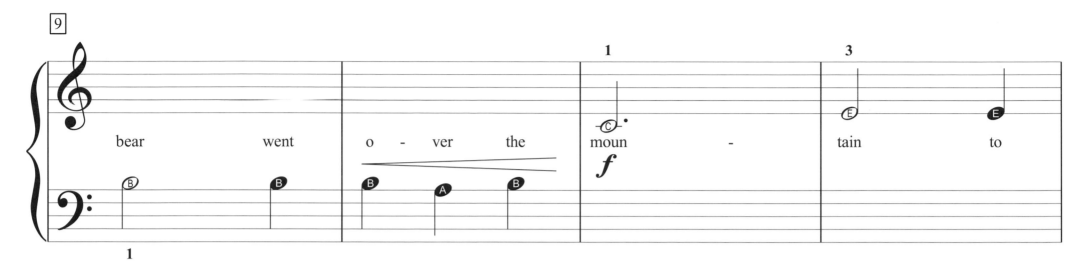

bear went o - ver the moun - tain to

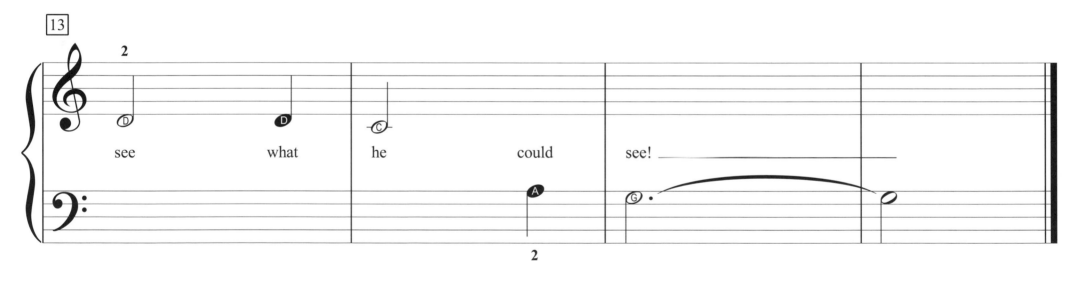

see what he could see!

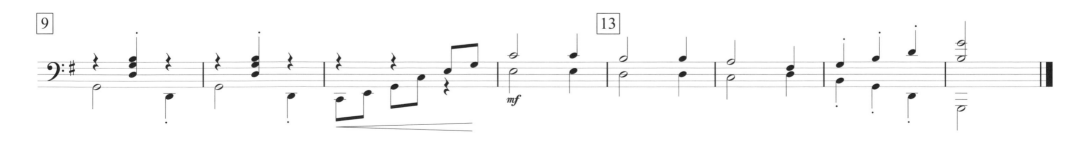

Kum Ba Yah

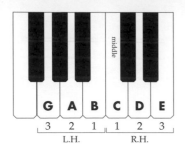

Traditional Spiritual
Arranged by Jennifer Linn

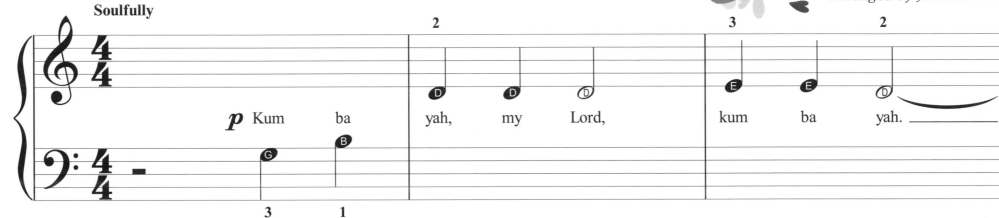

Soulfully

Soulfully

p Kum ba yah, my Lord, kum ba yah. _____

Kum ba yah, my Lord, kum ba yah. _____

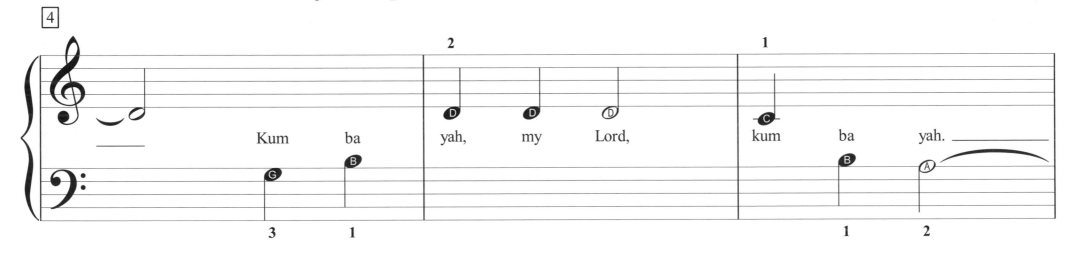

Accompaniment (Student plays one octave higher than written.)

Soulfully

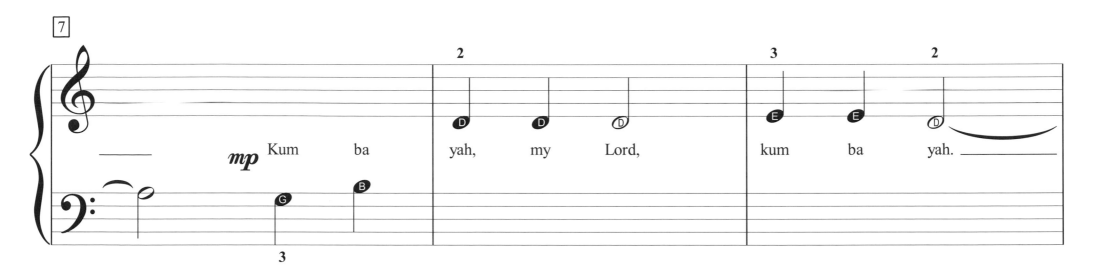

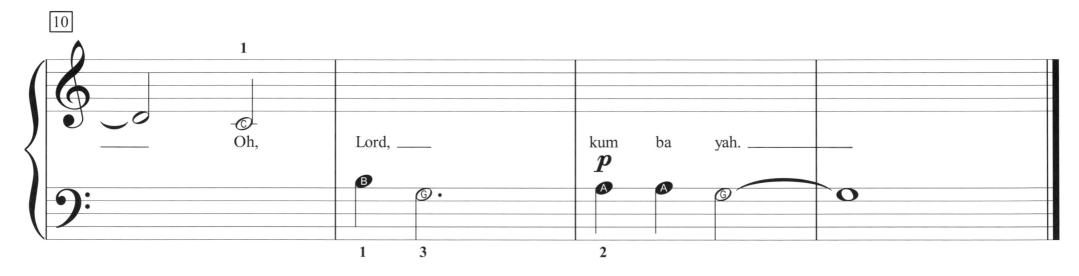

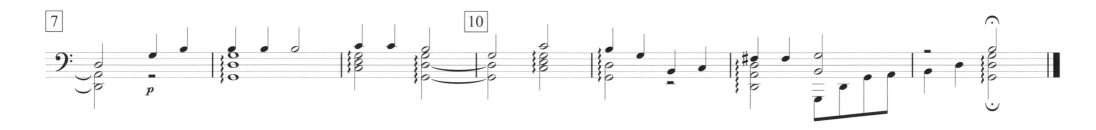

Jasmine Flower
(Mò Li Huã)

Chinese Folk Song
Arranged by Jennifer Linn

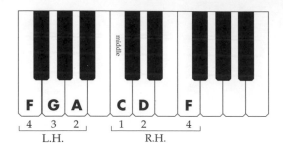

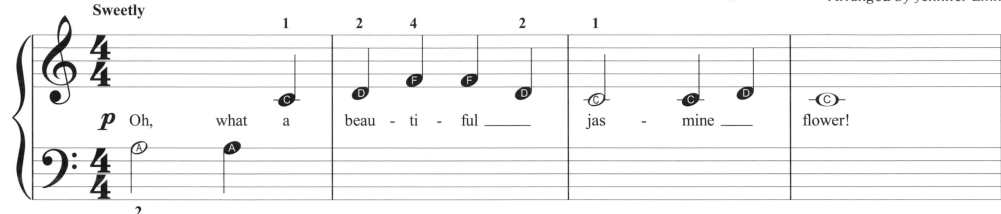

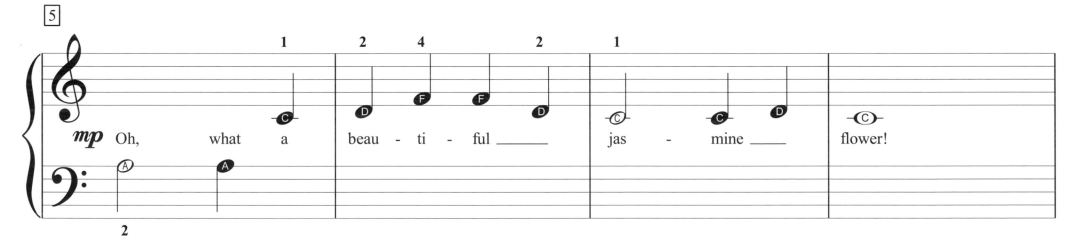

Accompaniment (Student plays one octave higher than written.)

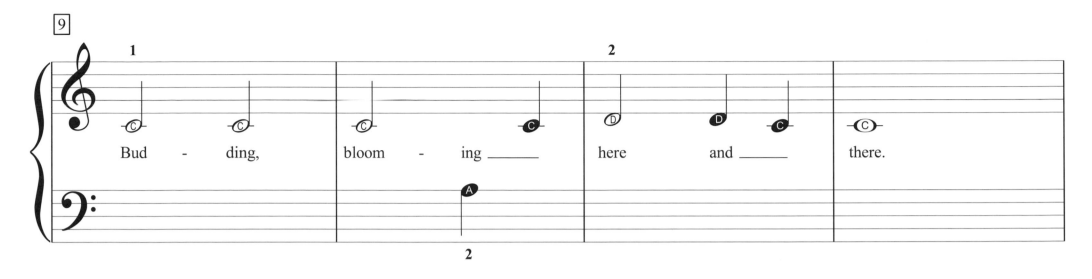

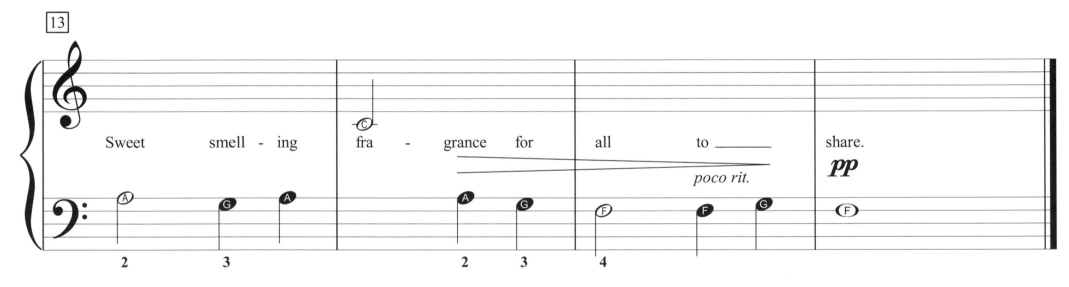

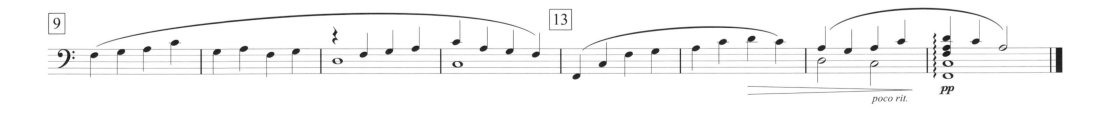

Secret Cave

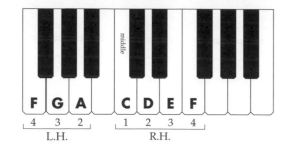

Words and Music by
Jennifer Linn

Mysteriously

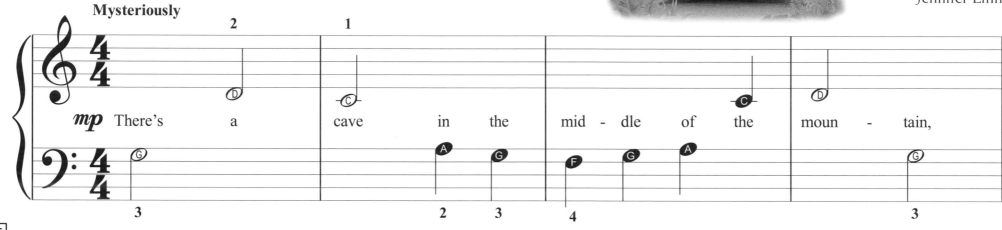

mp There's a cave in the mid - dle of the moun - tain,

hid - den deep in the Am - a - zon.

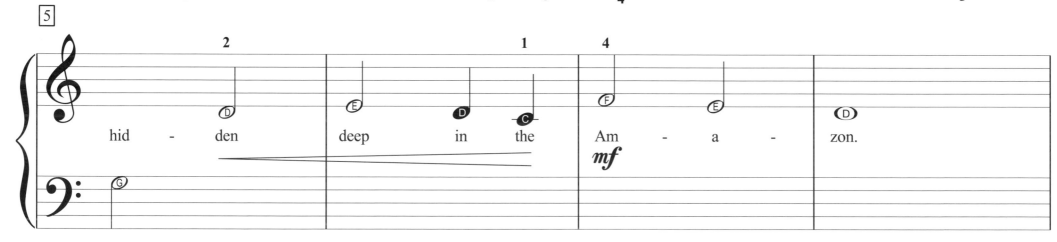

Accompaniment (Student plays as written.)
Mysteriously

p with pedal

mp

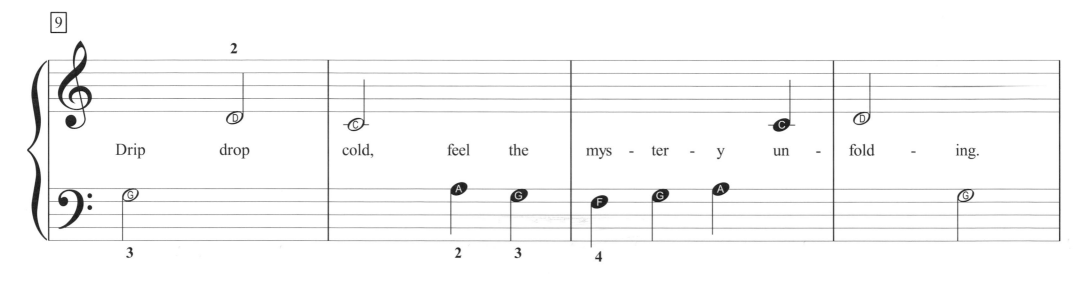

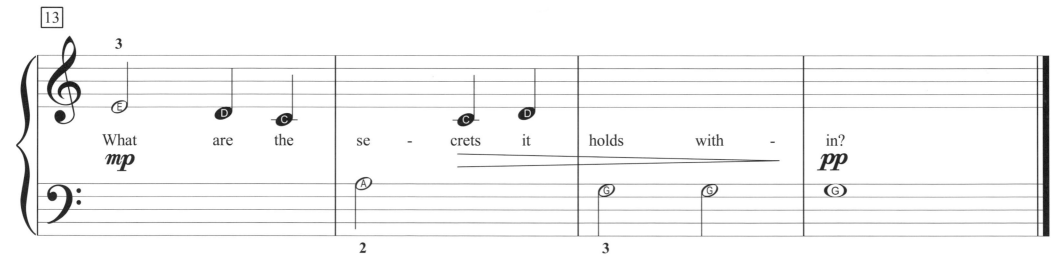